A PLACE APART

Houses of Christian Hospitality
and
Prayer in Europe

CYPRUS – GREECE – TURKEY

Janet L. Joy

Raphael Publishing
P.O. Box 750
Milton, WA 98354

Michael the Archangel drawing and prayer, page 79, courtesy of *The Franciscans*, St. Louis, MO.

The publisher is grateful for permission to use the artwork of Poor Clare Nuns. Note cards with similar artwork may be ordered by writing to:

Poor Clare Monastery of Our Lady of Guadalupe
800 East Nineteenth Street
Roswell, New Mexico 88201

Greek translations by Elly Pangis.

Library of Congress Catalog Number: 99-95457

ISBN: 0-9673074-1-4

RAPHAEL PUBLISHING
P.O. Box 750
Milton, WA 98354

Printed and bound in the United States of America

INTRODUCTION

A PLACE APART – Cyprus – Greece – Turkey – is a selection of monasteries that extend Christian hospitality to pilgrims that is in keeping with the ancient customs of Orthodox monasticism. One who is near an Orthodox monastery is welcome to call or visit and may share in what God provides at the time.

Most monasteries are open to pilgrims, and there is no formal structure of scheduled fees, tariffs, or formal retreat talks. This informal and simple arrangement has usually worked well for approximately a millennium, and pilgrims have found it practical and convenient.

Monasteries equipped with sufficient numbers of guest rooms receive pilgrims for overnight stays; otherwise, they are welcome for day visits.

This guidebook also lists a few Roman Catholic Guest Houses, but the listings are predominantly Orthodox.

The short essay on Mt. Athos was proofread by a monk on the Holy Mountain, and he updated my listings of the monasteries. It was a privilege and a blessing to receive his assistance, given as a true Brother in Christ.

May God Bless those of you who seek and find these havens of God's Peace and Love.

Janet L. Joy

MT. ATHOS – HOLY MOUNTAIN

Mount Athos rises six thousand feet above sea level and extends out into the Aegean Sea in northeastern Greece. With its craggy cliffs and pristine forests, the mountainous terrain is extremely rugged, and Mt. Athos is unattainable from the north. Access is by sea alone.

A bus can be taken from Thessaloniki to Ouranoupolis, a three hour ride. A Letter of Introduction is issued in Ouranoupolis before one can board the ferryboat to Dafni, the port of Athos, two hours away.

Dafni consists of a wharf, a few buildings, customs, and a shore policeman who checks a visitor's Letter of Introduction and Passport before allowing him to come to shore.

Only men are allowed on the Holy Mountain, and they must have an appropriate reason for visiting. Men closely connected with a religious or educational institution are looked upon with favor. Foreign visitors need to contact the Ministry of Macedonia and Thraki for permission to visit.

Dafni has a small hospice with very simple accommodations and food service.

Eighty per cent of the Holy Mountain is now accessible by road appropriate for motorized vehicles, or one may rent a mule – 'Athos Jeep'.

Once at the monastery of his choice, a guest will be assigned a simple cell. Meals, mostly vegetarian, are usually taken in a small guest dining room.

The views from Mt. Athos are spectacular and will not only be a blessing for visitors but will produce lasting memories.

Today all monasteries of Athos are cenobitic – the monks live in Community and share everything. They are obligated to attend religious services at set times.

There are approximately eighteen hundred monks on Mt. Athos, and about half live in monasteries. The remainder reside in sketes – small houses that surround a central church.

A few hermit monks live in caves on the south side of the Mountain. These vertical caves are accessed by scaling the face of the cliff on a chain. The monks from the monasteries furnish them with basic supplies.

The monastic day consists of praising God in prayer and chanting, obedience, fasting and work.

Life on Mt. Athos has changed little since 963 when the oldest monastery, and the one closest to the Holy Mountain, was founded – the Grand Lavra (Megistis Lavras).

Men seeking to visit some of the monasteries on Mt. Athos need an official Letter of Recommendation from an ecclesiastical authority or an educational institution. Then they must apply in writing, giving specific reasons for wanting to visit the Holy Mountain, and forward this, with the Letter of Recommendation to: Ministry of Macedonia and Thraki
Thessaloniki
GREECE
Tel: 031 257 010 (foreign visitors)

Cyprus

Ayia Napa Conference Center Tel: 03 721284
P. O. Box 30048   Fax: 03 722584
5340 Ayia Napa, Cyprus   Contact: Director
Ecumenical
E-mail:meccnapa@spidernet.com.cy

Open To: Individuals, groups for Conferences, Meetings of a spiritual, educational or cultural nature for study, reflection and prayer in an atmosphere of peace and beauty. Staff available to assist with planning program activities, and the Center can make arrangements for excursions within Cyprus with advance notice. All are welcome.

Accommodation: Hospitality is provided in 16 double rooms with private baths. Conference hall, meeting rooms, dining room. Contact for current rates.

Guests Admitted To: Orthodox Church along the courtyard. Library. Grounds.

Of Interest: Ayia Napa Conference Center is situated in the 15th c. Ayia Napa Monastery, no longer in active use, but made available by the late Archbishop Makarios and the Orthodox Church of Cyprus for use as an ecumenical conference center. It is administered by a Board of Management representing different Christian traditions: Orthodox Church of Cyprus, Armenian Apostolic Church, Episcopal Church of Jerusalem and the Middle East, Roman Catholic Church, and Maronite Church. The Center overlooks the Mediterranean, a half mile away – an area of fine sandy beaches and rock coves. Christians and non-Christians alike may wish to take longer excursions to places associated with the development of the Church from Biblical times.

Access: Air: Larnaca International Airport 50 km., then by taxi or bus. The Center can arrange appropriate transport from the airport with advance notice. Athens 90 min. by air.

Holy Royal and Stavropegic Monastry of the Panayia of Kykkos
Kykkos   Contact: Guest Brother
Cyprus
Greek Orthodox

Open To: Pilgrims wishing to visit the most famous monastery in Cyprus. Special Feastday: The Birth of the Theotokos (Mother of God) – Sept. 8th.

Accommodation: Hospitality is provided in comfortable rooms in the newly-built Guest House.

Guests Admitted To: Church where the miracle-working icon of the Holy Virgin of Kykkos has been safely kept since the 11th c. According to tradition, it was painted by St. Luke the Apostle. Museum. Library. Reception rooms.

Of Interest: Throughout the nine hundred year history of Kykkos Monastery, the monks have dedicated their lives to prayer and the ascetic life. The Brotherhood has a history of being active in the struggles for national liberation. They have made extensive social and cultural contributions to Cyprus, and have preserved the historical and Orthodox consciousness of the Cypriot people despite difficult times. The monastery maintains the only seminary in Cyprus. It has played significant roles in agriculture, tree cultivation, gardening, vine-growing and apiculture.

Access: Road: Passable. Mt. Olympus 18 km. Located on the W side of the Troodos Mountain Range.

Greece

Agias Ekaterinis Aeginis
Palea Hora Aeginis
Aegina, Greece
Greek Orthodox

Tel: 0297 22924
Contact: Mother Superior

Open To: Women for Private Retreat or simply for a few days of peace and quiet in a monastic setting. Pilgrims for day visits.

Accommodation: Hospitality is provided in the monastery.

Guests Admitted To: Monastery Church (1961). Special Feastday: St. Catherine – Nov. 25th. The public should contact the Sisters for schedule of services open to visitors.

Of Interest: Aegina is the hometown of St. Dionysios, who was confessor to the Sisters whose followers founded St. Catherine's Monastery in 1921. Historically, inhabitants of Aegina suffered ongoing persecution at the hands of pirates and the Turks. Each family built a small church as a shrine to a favorite saint and prayed for protection. The Hill of Churches, a special place of pilgrimage across from the monastery, has fourty small churches remaining of the three hundred and sixty. The Sisters and the faithful are caretakers. At the turn of the century, St. Nektarios, confessor to these Sisters, told them that one day this place would be glorified. A year after his death, they were able to build their monastery in honor of St. Catherine. It is under the administration of St. Nektarios Monastery.

Access: By boat from the mainland, then by car or on foot. Road: On the same road as St. Nektarios Monastery. The Island of Aegina is 14.4 km. long and is located in the Saronic Gulf off the SE coast of Greece.

Pallesviako
Iero Proskinima
Tis Yperagias
Theotokou
81101 Agiasou
Island of Lesvou, Greece

Open To: Pilgrims/visitors.

Accommodation: None.

Guests Admitted To: Church of Agiasou (1815), dedicated to the Dormition of the Mother of God. Special Feastday: Aug. 15th.

Of Interest: During iconoclastic times, the monk Agathon O. Efesios brought the great icon of Panagia from Jerusalem to Agiasou. It was originally named 'Icon of Agia Sion', which led to the shorter 'Agiasou'. It was housed at a monastery in Karya until a church was built in 1170, and later replaced by the present church.

Access: Road: Located at the foot of Mt. Olympos, 27 km. from Mytilini, the capital of Lesbos.

The Monastery of St. Theodosios the New
Iera Moni   Tel: 0752 44 240
Ocios Theodosios   Contact: Superior Mother of the Cloister
21055 Agia Trias
Nafplias – Argolis, Greece
Greek Orthodox
Sisterhood of St. Theodosius

Open To: Pilgrims seeking a special place of prayer. Visitors will be inspired by the spiritual virtues of silence, inner peace, and simplicity as exemplified by the Nuns, who place total faith and trust in God.

Accommodation: Hospitality is provided for 2 to 3 persons at a time on the west side of the monastery in restored cells.

Guests Admitted To: Church of St. Theodosius (larger church) and Church of the Transfiguration of Our Lord (Byzantine style – 11th c.) – one of the rare twin (dichoros) churches in Greece. Library. Reception Hall. Chapel of St. John the Baptist (exterior courtyard – 10th c.). Tomb of St. Theodosios. Cave Hermitage – restored into small Chapel of the Holy Cross. Chapel of Holy Meeting (on hill near monastery). Chapel dedicated to the Annunciation of the Blessed Virgin Mary (newest building, north of monastery).

Of Interest: Although desolate for centuries, citizens of Argolis venerated this hallowed ground. Between 1939 – 1942 restoration of the buildings began, and nuns from Athens were brought here to refound the monastery. Relics of St. Theodosios are kept in a silver case beside his icon. He was inspired by the ascetic and spiritual life of St. John the Baptist, and the buildings he constructed at Morea were very simple. Special Feastdays: The Transfiguration of Our Lord – Aug. 6th, and the Death of St. Theodosios – Aug. 7th.

Access: Road: Located between Nauplion and Argos near the villages of Panariti and Merbaca.

Monastery of Ypsoseos Timiou Stavrou   Tel: 0321 91353
TK62051 Agiou Pnevma Serron
Greek Orthodox

Open To: Pilgrims, visitors who wish a short stay in a peaceful setting.

Accommodation: Hospitality is provided for one night only.

Guests Admitted To: Small Byzantine-style Church, dedicated to the Holy Cross. Special Feastday: The Elevation of the Cross – Sept. 14th.

Of Interest: The Monastery of the Elevation of the Holy Cross is a small women's monastery built in 1964 by the villagers following a pious man's dream to erect a small church here. Two nuns have resided here since 1985. Relics kept here are those of St. Gregory V, St. Nicholas, St. Philothei of Athens, St. John the Baptist, and St. Anysia. There is also a fragment of the Holy Cross as well as the blood of St. Philoumenos of Jerusalem.

Access: Road: Located near the village of Agio Pnevma (Holy Spirit), 15 km. NE of Serres through the National Road. The Monastery of the Prophet Elias is 3 km. away.

Agia Varvara Amaliados
27200 Amaliada
Greece
Greek Orthodox
Holy Metropolis Eleias

Open To: Visitors, pilgrims wishing to view the church.

Accommodation: None.

Guests Admitted To: Small Byzantine-style Church.
Grounds.

Of Interest: Around 1960, an Orthodox Nun had a dream that
she was to build a church on this site. In time, she managed to
receive enough donations from neighbors and pilgrims to realize
her dream. The lot was given to her, and she was the only
resident and caretaker. Present conditions are uncertain.

Access: Road: Head E past fields, woods and small houses.
Located 1 km. from Frangavilla.

Agios Athanasios Kouroutas   Tel: 06 22 27 306
TK27200 Amaliada   Contact: Guest Sister
Greece
Greek Orthodox
Holy Metropolis of Eleias

Open To: Pilgrims/visitors. Closed during winter.

Accommodation: Hospitality is provided for a few guests for one night.

Guests Admitted To: Monastery Church, dedicated to St. Athanasios. Grounds.

Of Interest: This lovely women's monastery was built in 1920 and is situated near the seashore in an area of fine homes and villas. The grounds are lush with flowers and other vegetation. Visitors will appreciate the many beautiful icons.

Access: Road: From the shore, turn right, pass a campground, then right again, and left. The monastery has a distinctive red-tiled roof and is situated at the end of a straight stretch of road. Located near the village of Kourouta Amaliados.

Agios Nektarios Amaliados
27200 Amaliada
Greece
Greek Orthodox
Holy Metropolis of Eleias

Open To: Pilgrims/visitors.

Accommodation: None at the monastery.

Guests Admitted To: Church of St. Nektarios for liturgical
services.

Of Interest: The monastery was built in 1970 in a greenbelt.
It runs a sewing school for girls. Visitors will find the liturgical
music and chants spiritually uplifting.

Access: Road: Dirt road for a short distance. Located in city of
Amaliada.

Agiou Athanasiou Ampelokampou
TK27200 Amaliada
Greece
Greek Orthodox
Holy Metropolis of Eleias

Tel: 06 22 61 280
Contact: Guest Sister

Open To: Pilgrims/visitors.

Accommodation: Hospitality is provided for guests for one night.

Guests Admitted To: Monastery Church, dedicated to St. Athanasios. Special Feastday: Jan. 18th. Grounds.

Of Interest: This women's retreat monastery was originally a men's monastery, founded in 1894. Many monks lost their lives during the Revolution of 1821 for assisting resistance fighters. The small church and monastery house many icons and ancient holy paintings. Water from the well is reputed to have healing effects.

Access: Rail: To Ampelokampos. Road: 1 km. from Gastouni, turn toward Ampelokampos.

Frangavillas Monastery   Tel: 06 22 28 994
27200 Amaliada
Greece
Greek Orthodox
Holy Metropolis Eleias

Open To: Pilgrims, visitors coming to pay homage to Our
Blessed Mother (Theotokos), and for those wishing to spend
time in a 'house of prayer'.

Accommodation: Hospitality is provided in a few guest rooms
for one night.

Guests Admitted To: Byzantine-style Church dedicated to
Panagia (Blessed Virgin Mary), for worship services. Special
Feastdays: Aug. 15th and the 2nd day following Easter Sunday.
Grounds.

Of Interest: This men's monastery, founded in the 11th c., is
named after a Frank who built a villa on a nearby hill. Franks
lived in the area from the 1200's to the 1400's, and at one time
the church was Roman Catholic. The faithful saved the majestic
Byzantine icon of Theotokos from destruction during the wars
that plagued this land. The grounds of the monastery and
surrounding area are lush with vegetation, and the vista is
grand.

Access: Road: 2 ½ km. from Amaliada.

Isihastirio Agiou Dimitriou
Amaliados
TK27200 Amaliada, Greece
Greek Orthodox
Holy Metropolis of Eleias

Tel: 06 22 28 961
Contact: Guest Sister

Open To: Pilgrims wishing to spend a time apart for spiritual renewal in an environment of peace and hospitality.

Accommodation: Hospitality is provided for one night.

Guests Admitted To: Monastery Church, dedicated to St. Dimitrios. Grounds.

Of Interest: This women's monastery, built in 1930, is set in lovely grounds with beautiful scenery near the city of Amaliados.

Access: Rail: Disembark at Kardamas, then 1 km. on foot to monastery.

Monastery Analipseos Zerou
Geraki
27200 Amaliada, Greece
Greek Orthodox
Holy Metropolis of Eleias

Tel: 06 22 28 150
Contact: Guest Sister

Open To: Pilgrims/visitors.

Accommodations: Hospitality is provided in the monastery's guest rooms for a few visitors for one night.

Guests Admitted To: Church, dedicated to the Ascension of Our Lord Jesus Christ. Grounds.

Of Interest: This women's monastery, built in 1935, is set in lovely surroundings near the city.

Access: Road: Yeraki 4 km. Amaliada 6 km.

Prophetou Eliou Amaliados
TK27200 Amaliada
Greece
Greek Orthodox
Holy Metropolis of Eleias

Tel: 06 22 28 442
Contact: Guest Sister

Of Interest: Visitors wishing to learn more about this monastery, and for those needing a short retreat.

Accommodation: Hospitality is provided for a few guests for one night.

Guests Admitted To: Monastery Church, dedicated to the Prophet Elias. Special Feastday: July 20th. Grounds.

Of Interest: This monastery, built in 1920, has many beautiful icons of saints and the Prophet Elias.

Access: Road: Amaliada 1 km.

Ieros Naos Agiou Nikolaou   Tel: (0681) 26138 or 22417
TK47100 Arta
Greece
Greek Orthodox

Open To: Pilgrims/visitors.

Accommodation: None on church grounds.

Guests Admitted To: Byzantine-style Church of Agia Theodora (13th c.), dedicated to the wife of Duke Michil II. This church replaced Agios Georgios at the Monastery of St. George where Theodora lived as a nun after the death of her husband. Her special feastday is celebrated Mar. 11th, and her tomb is at the church.

Of Interest: Arta is built on seven hills on the site of ancient Ambrakia. Other places of religious significance are the Church of Parigoritissa, the Church of Agios Basilios, and the Monastery of Kato Panagia. Arta is near the beautiful beach hotels of Preveza. Agia Theodora is in the western part of town.

Access: Road: Located on the River Arachtos, 17 km. from Ambrakikos Bay.

Monastery Iesodion Theotokou Melissourgon
47100 Arta   Tel: 0681 23933
Greece   Fax: 0681 28610
Greek Orthodox

Open To: Pilgrims/visitors.

Accommodation: Only in Hotel Tzoumerka – 4 km.

Guests Admitted To: Monastery Church.

Of Interest: This men's monastery was built in 1821, and at
one time operated a school. The monastery is an annex of Kato
Panagias Nunnery in Arta. It is set in a peaceful but rugged
landscape, surrounded by mountain peaks, with breathtaking
panoramic views.

Access: Road: Located in the village of Melissourgoi in NW
Greece, N of the Ambracian Gulf. Arta 70 km. Athens 450 km.

Foyer d'Accueil 'Divine Providence' Tel: 9221002
30, rue Aminokleous, Neos Kosmos Fax: 9220114
11744 Athens, Greece Contact: Guest Sister
Byzantine Rite Catholic

Open To: The Sisters welcome guests seeking to stay in a
Christian environment. Advance reservations necessary.

Accommodation: Hospitality is provided in two houses in
comfortably furnished rooms (75 beds).

Guests Admitted To: Small Chapel. Garden area. Byzantine
Rite Catholic Church – Pammakaristou Theotokou.

Of Interest: The House of Divine Providence was founded over
fifty years ago as a residence for working girls and students. It
now includes lodging for students and visitors from abroad. At
the time of their 50th anniversary in 1994, the Sisters had
housed 8650 Greek girls and hosted 32,000 foreign visitors. The
Sisters wish to enrich the lives of others by instructing them
regarding archaeological and historical sites in Greece and
abroad, and they are available to act as tour guides if requested.
Foyer d'Accueil is close to the Acropolis and Areios Pagos where
the Apostle Paul preached.

Access: Contact for further information.

The Sacred Convent of Malevi   Tel: 0792 31243
Agios Petros   Contact: Guest Sister
Cynouria, Greece
Greek Orthodox

Open To: Pilgrims and retreatants, both residential and non-residential visits.

Accommodation: Hospitality is provided in the Guest House in pleasant, sunny rooms southeast of the Convent.

Guests Admitted To: Church for liturgical services and private devotion before the holy icon of Our Lady of the Angels. Chapel of St. Neilos which houses his relics. Exhibition Hall. Gardens.

Of Interest: According to tradition, the first monastery dates back to 717. It was transferred to the present location in 1616. In 1949, nuns took it over and have done much restoration work. They have farm animals, a large vineyard, and an olive grove. Tradition claims that the miraculous icon is one of those seventy painted by Luke the Evangelist and brought by the inhabitants of Mt. Athos who settled in Cynouria.

Access: Road: Located near St. Peter (Agios Petros) about 30 km. from Astros and 45 km. from Tripolis.

Monasteries on Mt. Athos
63087 Dafni
Greece

Megistis Lavra – established in 963 from Agios Athanasios.
Tomb of St. Athanasios. Famous icon from 1713 – Panagia
Koukouzelissas. Relics include staff of St. Athanasios. Several
small monasteries surround it. Located in eastern part of
peninsula, 35 km. from Karyes, 30 km. from Agia Annis, 17 ½
km. from Karakalou. One hour by mule from Kafsokalivia
Skete. Access by boat, auto, foot, mule.

Vatopediou – established between 972-980 by the monks
Athanasio Nikolaos and Antonios. Relics include holy belt of the
Theotokos; skull of St. Gregory the Theologian. Located near
the water in northern part of peninsula. First visible monastery
along the coast. 15 km. from Karyes, 10 km. from
Pantokratoras, 12 ½ km. from Esfigmenou. Access by boat,
auto, foot, mule.

Iviron – original monastery built in 1030; present one
established in 1972. Retains many traditions including keeping
time according to Chaldaic system – sunrise being zero hour.
The other monasteries on Athos start at sunset – Byzantine
system. The vigil light in front of the Holy Doors of the church
sways back and forth if any form of danger is at hand. Located
near the water in northern part of peninsula, 7 ½ km. from
Karyes. Access by boat, car, foot, mule.

Hiliandariou – established in 1197 by the Serbians, St.
Symeon and his son St. Savva. Their tombs are here. Vineyard
considered miraculous regarding petitions for fertility problems.
Icon of Panagia with three hands, responsible for miraculous
cure of St. John of Damascene. Located in northern part of
peninsula 30 km. from Karyes. Access by boat, auto, foot, mule.

Agiou Dionysiou – established in 1389 by St. Dionysiou from Korytsa, Albania. Located in northern part of peninsula near the water, 80 m. above sea level, 20 km. from Karyes. Access by boat, auto, foot, mule.

Koutloumousiou – established the end of the 12th c. Small monastery. Located 500 m. from Karyes. Access by boat, auto, foot, mule.

Pantokrotoros – established in 1363 by brothers Asanous, Palaiologous, Alexios, and Ioannis. Located in northern part of peninsula near the water, a short distance down the coast from Vatopediou. 30 m. above sea level, 7 ½ km. from Karyes. Access by boat, auto, foot, mule.

Xiropotamou – established in 970 by St. Pavlos Xiropotaminos. Located in northern part of peninsula, 10 km. from Karyes, 2 ½ km. from Dafni. Access by boat, auto, foot, mule.

Zografou – Bulgarian, established in 972 by brothers Moses, Aaron, and John from town of Ahrida. They were indecisive about name for the monastery so they left a plain white board. In time, the icon of St. George appeared on the board. Thus, Zografou, meaning painter. Located 17 ½ km. from Karyes. Access by boat, auto, foot, mule.

Doheiariou – established in the 10th or 11th c. by the monk Euthymio, whose job was to fill containers. Doheiariou means vessel. This is the first monastery one comes to. Located in northern part of peninsula, 30 m. above sea level, 15 km. from Karyes, 10 km. from Dafni. Access by boat, foot, mule.

Karakallou – established in the 11th c. by the monk Nikolaos Karakallos. Beautiful tower, built by one of the monks in 1534. Located in northern part of peninsula, 100 m. above sea level, 17 ½ km. from Karyes. Access by boat, auto, foot, mule.

Filotheou – established in 990 by Filotheos. Relics include right hand of St. John Chrysostomos. Located in northern part of peninsula, 300 m. above sea level, 12 ½ km. from Karyes. Access by boat, auto, foot, mule.

Simonos Petras – established in 1364. Its construction is the most daring on Holy Athos, set on a high pinnacle. Located in northern part of peninsula, 230 m. above sea level, 17 ½ km. from Karyes, 10 km. from Dafni. Access by boat, auto, foot, mule.

Agiou Pavlou – established in the 10th c. by St. Xiropotaminos. Relics include two large pieces of the Holy Cross and the Holy Gifts presented to Jesus by the Wise Men. Located in northern part of peninsula, 25 km. from Karyes, 20 km. from Dafni. Access by boat, auto, foot, mule.

Stavronikita – established in 1541. Small monastery. Icon of St. Nicholas, was in the sea for 500 years, found by the monks. An oyster adheres to it – named 'St. Nicholas of the Oyster Icon'. Access by boat, auto, foot, mule.

Osiou Xenofontos – established in the 11th c. by Pius Xenofon. One of the largest monasteries on the Holy Mountain. Relics include piece of the Holy Cross; relic of the first Christian martyr, St. Stephanos. Located in northern part of peninsula, 15 km. from Karyes, 7 ½ km. from Dafni. Access by boat, foot, mule.

Osiou Grigoriou – established in the 14th c. by Gregory Sinaiti. Relics include piece of the Holy Cross; two feet and right hand of St. Anastasia the Roman. Miraculous icons of Panagia the Guide and Panagia Galaktotrofousa. Located in northern part of peninsula, 20 km. from Karyes, 12 ½ km. from Dafni. Access by boat, auto, foot, mule.

Esfigmenou – established in the 10th c. Name derives from the fact that it is encircled by mountains. Some claim it derives from the first monk who wore his belt too tight. Relics include left foot of St. Panteleimon. Located in northern part of peninsula, 25 km. from Karyes. Access by boat, foot, mule.

Agiou Panteleimonos – Russian, established in the 12th c. Newest monastery on Athos. Huge bell tower. Monastery can accommodate up to 1800 persons for day visits. Relics include some of the Apostles Peter, Andrew, Matthew, Luke, Thomas and Bartholomew. Located in northern part of peninsula near the water, at an elevation of 30 m., 15 km. from Karyes, 2 ½ km. from Dafni. Access by boat, foot, mule.

Konstamonitou – established in the 11th c. by a monk named Konstamonitis. Located in northern part of peninsula, 200 m. above sea level, 15 km. from Karyes, 15 km. from Dafni. Access by boat, foot, mule.

Skiti Agias Annis – established in the 16th c. Relic of right foot of St. Anna, Mother of the Blessed Virgin Mary. Steep climb. Located 30 km. from Megistis Lavra. Access by boat, foot, mule.

Nea Skiti – established in 1760 by Agiou Pavlou. Access by boat, foot, mule.

Mikra Agia Anna – established by Skiti Agias Annis. Ten small houses at a higher elevation than Skiti Agias Annis. The famous hymnographos Gerasimos Mikrayiannonitis lived here for years. Located in northern part of peninsula. Access by boat, foot, mule.

Kavsokalyvia – artist monks live in sketes. Located 12 ½ km. from Agia Annis and Megistis Lavra. Access by boat, foot, mule.

Karoulia – name means pulley. Hermit monks reside in cells in caves of steep ledges. A place of solitude amidst desert and rocky terrain. Located past Agia Anna. Access by boat, foot, mule.

Timiou Prodromou – Romanian, established in 1820 by two Romanian monks. Dedicated to St. John the Forerunner. Located 25 m. above sea level. Access by boat, foot, mule.

Skiti Karyes – the capital of Holy Mountain. Metropolitan Church of Holy Mountain (10th c.), called Protaton. Seat of Holy Community of Mount Athos (a type of government). Miracle-working icon of Axion Estin in Protato. Access by car, foot, mule.

Skiti Agiou Andreou (Sarai) – large Russian buildings and the largest church of Holy Mountain. A part of the skiti is now the Athonias Ekklesiastic Academy, a school originally for monks – now for children desiring religious studies. Access by car, foot, mule.

Ano Moni Hrysopigi   Tel: 06 2481 263
TK27063 Divris   Contact: Guest Brother
Lampeia, Greece
Greek Orthodox
Holy Metropolis of Eleias

Open To: Pilgrims, visitors for retreats or simply a time apart in a spiritual place of peace and beauty.

Accommodation: Hospitality is provided in the monastery Guest House.

Guests Admitted To: Monastery Church, dedicated to the Birth of Theotokos. Special Feastday: Sept. 8th. Grounds.

Of Interest: The monastery, built in 1674, has many holy paintings and frescoes. During the Revolution of 1821 between the Greeks and Turks, the monks conducted a secret school in the basement of the northwest part of the monastery.

Access: Road: Through the ancient city of Olympia and the Folois Forest. Located 60 km. from Pyrgos near the village of Lampeia, northwest Peloponnesus, southern Greece.

Holy Monastery of Saints Avgoustinou Ippanos
and Serafeim Tou Sarof   Tel: 0634 44 282
Trikorfo Doridos   Fax: 0634 44 390
33056 Efpalio, Greece
Greek Orthodox

Open To: Individuals, groups who wish to join the monks for
worship services. Day visits. Year round.

Accommodation: None at the monastery. Inquire about
possibility of lodging at a nearby women's monastery.

Guests Admitted To: Byzantine-style Church, dedicated to St.
Avgoustinou Ippanos and St. Serafeim Tou Sarof. Special
Feastdays: June 15th and July 19th.

Of Interest: This new monastery was founded in 1992 by
Archimandrite Nektarios Moulatsiotis.

Access: By road.

Koimisis Theokou Kryonerion
27069 Ephyra
Greece
Greek Orthodox
Holy Metropolis Eleias

Open To: Visitors wishing to view the outside of the monastery
which is closed.

Guests Admitted To: Grounds.

Of Interest: This small monastery was last inhabited by nuns.
The church is dedicated to Koimisis Theotokou. Special
Feastday: Aug. 23rd. The Monastery of Analipseos Yerakiou is
nearby.

Access: Road: Winding, gravel and dirt. Located near the
village of Kryoneri, Amaliados District.

Moni Zoothohou Pigis
TK27058 Epitalio
Greece
Greek Orthodox
Holy Metropolis Triphyllias – Olympias

Open To: Pilgrims/visitors.

Accommodation: None.

Guests Admitted To: Church. Grounds.

Of Interest: The monastery was built in this century. Visitors
will be impressed with the natural beauty of the area and the
peace surroundings. There are lovely views of the sea and of
Kyparissia to the Katakolo.

Access: Road: Epitalio 2 km.

Moni Katholikis Gastounis
TK27300 Gastouni
Greece
Greek Orthodox
Holy Metropolis Eleias

Open To: Pilgrims/visitors wishing to view the famous icon of
Theotokous. Day visits only.

Guests Admitted To: Church (10th c.), dedicated to the
Dormition of Theotokos – magnificent Byzantine Icon of
Theotokous. Grounds.

Of Interest: Visitors will sense the sacred in this holy, ancient
place despite the fact that the wall paintings are unclear. The
church is full of holy paintings that are faded from the ages and
the plunder of barbarians.

Access: Road: Located at the edge of the city of Gastounis.

Holy Monastery Epanosifi   Contact: Abbot
70010 Irakleion
Island of Crete, Greece
Greek Orthodox

Open To: Individuals, families, groups wishing to visit the
monastery and church, and for those seeking a place for
spiritual retreat.

Accommodation: Hospitality is provided in monastic guest
quarters.

Guests Admitted To: Church of Agios Georgio. Special
Feastdays: Apr. 23rd and Nov. 3rd. Library. Grounds.

Of Interest: Holy Monastery St. George was founded in 1590
by the monk Paisios. Over the centuries, the monks suffered
hardships and destruction when they joined the local citizenry
to resist tyranny from invading forces. Restoration efforts have
been ongoing. The monastery houses sacred relics of saints and
the magnificent Icon of St. George, painted in 1907.

Access: Road: Located 30 km. S of Irakleion, the main city on
the island. Near the village of Karkadiotissa and Metaxohori in
the District of Monofatsiou.

Monastery Panagias Kalyvianis   Tel: 089222151
70400 Irakleion
Kritis (Crete), Greece
Greek Orthodox

Open To: Individuals, groups wishing to attend Mass.

Guests Admitted To: Byzantine Church of Panagias – Tis
Kalyvianis (1911-1924), dedicated to the Dormition of
Theotokos.

Of Interest: This women's monastery was established in 1961
near the site of the small church built between 961-1000. In
1873 the miraculous Icon of the Annunciation of Theotokos was
found, and is held here in the wood carved holy icon stand. The
nuns are engaged in many social and religious works of love and
service to persons in need.

Access: Road: Located 60 km. from Iraklion near the village of
Kalyvia between Moires and Tympaki on the S side of the Island
of Crete.

Koimesis Theotokou   Tel: 0431 86255
Bytouma Kalampakas   Contact: Sr. Christodule
42200 Kalampaka, Greece
Greek Orthodox

Open To: Pilgrims for day visits.

Guests Admitted To: Small Convent Church (1600), dedicated to the Dormition of the Mother of God. Public welcome for the Divine Liturgy on Sundays.

Of Interest: According to tradition, an icon of the Blessed Virgin Mary was found in this area and named Panagia Kalampakiotissa after the town of Kalampaka. The oldest buildings of the holy Convent of the Mother of God Bytouma date from the 16th c. In 1952 the complex was taken over by Sisters from Patra. They remodeled the buildings and added new structures. In 1960 they established a school of arts and crafts.

Access: Road: Approx. 20 km. W of Trikala, close to Mt. Koziakas and the village of Bytouma.

Moni Sepetou
TK27062 Kallithea
Greece
Greek Orthodox
Holy Metropolis Triphyllias – Olympias

Open To: Pilgrims/visitors for day visits.

Guests Admitted To: Monastery Church. Grounds.

Of Interest: This impressive monastery was built in the 11th c. on a rock ledge overlooking the Triton River, a tributary of the Alfeios River. The monks played an active role in resisting tyranny during the Revolution of 1821.

Access: Road: From Andritsaina or from Olympia.

Agios Nikolaos Spata
Spata
TK25200 Kato Achaia, Greece
Greek Orthodox
Holy Metropolis Eleias

Open To: Pilgrims/visitors for day visits.

Guests Admitted To: Monastery Church with the miraculous Icon of St. Nikolas. Liturgy every Sunday. Special Feastday: May 10th to commemorate the passage of the saint's holy relics from Peloponessos coming from Myra of Lycia toward the city of Bari, Italy.

Of Interest: The Monastery of Holy Nikolas of Spata was founded in the 18th c.. St. Nikolas was Bishop of Myra of Lycia. Tradition states that the holy icon was found in a small cave at this location. The faithful began to come to venerate the sacred image, and a church was built on the spot. Thousands of pilgrims come barefoot on the saint's name day, walking the whole road. Having kept a strict fast, they come bearing gifts, as they seek a special favor from St. Nikolas. A barren tree located at Paliovryssis, the holy place in which the icon was found, is covered with strips of clothing tied to it by pilgrims wishing to leave something personal behind. Today the monastery also runs an orphanage.

Access: Road: Take Hwy. from Patras to Pyrgos. Located 17 km. E of city of Varda near village of Spata.

Holy Convent Panagia – Portaitissa
68400 Kornofolia   Tel: 0554 51111
Soufli, Greece   Contact: The Mother Superior
Greek Orthodox

Open To: Pilgrims/visitors.

Accommodation: Hospitality is provided in the guest
quarters. Meals taken separate from the nuns.

Guests Admitted To: Small Church to join the nuns for
liturgical services.

Of Interest: Tradition dates the convent back to the 16th c.,
and it is under the jurisdiction of the Monastery Iviron of Mt.
Athos. The miraculous Icon of Mary is a copy of the Icon of
Portaitissa of the Monastery Iviron. Monks brought the copy
here when the monastery became annexed in 1748. In 1980 this
monastery was restored by monks and became a women's
monastery, dedicated to the Dormition of the Mother of God.
The miraculous icons of the Virgin Mary and St. Haralampos
are in the small church, and the reliquary with a relic of the
right foot of St. Haralampos can also be found there.

Access: Road: The Monastery sets on the small hill named
Kouri, 1 km. from the town of Kornofolia, 5 km. from Soufli.
Located in the center of Province of Evrou about 1 hr. from city
of Alexandroupoli.

Isihastirion Timiou Prodromou   Contact: Guest Sister
85300 Kos
Island of Kos, Greece
Greek Orthodox
Holy Metropolis of Kos

Open To: Pilgrims wishing to visit the monastery for a short stay.

Accommodation: Hospitality is provided in the Guest House for overnight stays.

Guests Admitted To: Monastery Church. Five smaller churches surrounding the monastery.

Of Interest: This women's retreat was established in 1970 and is dedicated to the Holy Forerunner, St. John the Baptist. It was founded by Nathanail, the Metropolitan at that time.

Access: Road: Located near the villages of Zia and Asfendiou, approx. 13 km. from Kos.

Agios Nektarios   Contact: Guest Sister
85300 Kos
Island of Kos, Greece

Open To: Pilgrims for a short stay.

Accommodation: Hospitality is provided in guest quarters.

Guests Admitted To: Monastery Church of St. Nektarios.

Of Interest: This women's monastery was established in 1971. The church, completed in 1973, is in the shape of a cross. It was founded by Nathanail, the Metropolitan of Kos at that time, from the Holy Mountain Athos, Monastery of Lavras.

Access: Road: Passable.

Kato Panagias Vlahernas
TK27068 Kyllini
Greece
Greek Orthodox
Holy Metropolis Eleias

Open To: Pilgrims/visitors for day visits.

Guests Admitted To: Monastery Church for worship services
(a replica of an Orthodox Church in Constantinople – Panagias
Vlahernas). Church dedicated to Genesio Theotokos. Special
Feastday: Sept. 8th. Grounds – guests served refreshments
under the olive trees. Library.

Of Interest: The monastery was founded in the 12th c. and
later occupied by Franks and Latin monks, but it again became
Orthodox in 1628. It had many holy artifacts, relics of saints,
and icons. The monks suffered much during the Revolution.
Orthodox nuns occupied the monastery for a period of time.
During the 1920's, refugees were allowed to establish a home
here. At present, it functions as a home for the elderly and
disabled.

Access: Road/Rail: To Kyllini, then 2 ½ km. to the monastery.
Located in Kyllini Eleias near the village of Kato Panagia.

Monastery Koimiseos Theotokou Elonis
Leonithion   Tel: 0757 22297
22300 Kynourias, Greece
Greek Orthodox

Open To: Pilgrims/visitors.

Accommodation: Hospitality is provided in the monastery's
guest quarters.

Guests Admitted To: Monastery Church, with the miraculous
Icon of Theotokos, a masterpiece by St. Luke the Evangelist.
Special Feastday: Dormition of Theotokou – Aug. 15th.
Grounds.

Of Interest: Holy Monastery Elonis was probably built in the
16th c. after the discovery of the Icon of Theotokos by shepherds
when they spotted a light coming from the area. The
Metropolitan of the district entrusted the icon to two monks,
Kallikos and Dositheo. They built a small church and
monastery. Because of the many miracles that were taking
place here, the monastery became famous and grew in size.
Over time, it suffered under enemy nations. The monks
provided invaluable service to their country during the
Revolution of 1821. It became a women's monastery in 1971.

Access: Road: 17 km. through the city of Leonithion toward
village of Kosmas.

Koimiseos Theotokou Kremastis   Contact: Guest Sister
TK27064 Lanthion
Karatoulas, Greece
Greek Orthodox
Holy Metropolis Eleias

Open To: Pilgrims/visitors.

Accommodation: Hospitality is provided for a night's lodging
for a few guests.

Guests Admitted To: Monastery Church, dedicated to the
Dormition of the Theotokos. Special Feastday: Aug. 23rd.
Grounds.

Of Interest: One evening in the year 1200, shepherds saw a
light coming from a cave. They lowered a shepherd by rope
through the opening, and he found the Icon of Theotokos
hanging there. The monastery was built on a rocky prominence,
and visitors will marvel at the panoramic view of the whole
District of Eleias to the forest of Folois. The monks suffered
much during the Revolution of 1821. Since the 1930's, this has
been a women's monastery. Guests are welcome to view the
many holy artifacts.

Access: Road: The Road of Varvasaina, 18 km. from Pyrgos,
near Mt. Foloi and the villages of Lampeti and Lanthi, NW
Peloponnesus, southern Greece.

Agios Athanasios Lehainon
TK27053 Lechaina
Greece
Greek Orthodox
Holy Metropolis Eleias

Open To: Pilgrims/visitors for day visits.

Guests Admitted To: Small, brick Church. Grounds.

Of Interest: The Retreat of St. Athanasius, with its lovely yard, gardens and flowers, is situated near the seashore of Lehainon. Conditions at present are uncertain, for in recent years its caretaker has been an elderly nun (and her dogs).

Access: Road: Located 36 km. N of Pyrgos, 60 km. S of Patras on the W coast of Greece.

Holy Monastery Leimonos-Kalloni   Tel: 0253 22289
TK81107 Island of Lesbos
Greek Orthodox

Open To: Pilgrims/visitors for rest, renewal and study. Also, volunteers wishing to help with the work at the monastery, participating in monastic life.

Accommodation: Hospitality is provided in the guest quarters in 500 beds for varying lengths of time. Evening meal taken with the monks. Also, at 6 smaller monasteries administered by Limonos. Charming hermitages around Kaloni Lesvos.

Guests Admitted To: Monastery Church (1795), dedicated to Taxiarch Michael. Small Church of St. Ignatius (men only), dedicated to Koimisis of Theotokos. Special Feastday: Oct. 14th. Museum. Library. 16th c. cells. Cell of St. Ignatius.

Of Interest: St. Ignatius Agalliano is considered the founder of this men's monastery. The monastery has relics of many saints, and pilgrims have been welcomed for many years. It provides a framework in which visitors can learn about monastic life. There is also a home for the elderly with the small Church of St. Nikothimos. Nearby is the Church of the Five Virgins, situated on top of an old olive oil factory. Outside the dining room of the monastery is the small Church of St. Jacob.

Access: Road: Located 3 km. from town of Kalloni, at head of Gulf of Kalloni in center of island, on a beautiful plain. In E Aegean Sea off NW coast of Turkey.

Monastery of Evangelismos Theotokou Orous
Amomon Makri   Tel: 02 94 91 202
TK19005 Makri, Greece
Greek Orthodox

Open To: Pilgrims/visitors.

Accommodation: Hospitality is provided for one night only.

Guests Admitted To: Byzantine-style Church, dedicated to
Holy Efraim. Grounds.

Of Interest: This women's monastery was built between the
10th and 11th c., and was originally a men's monastery. It has
many holy paintings. Holy Efraim was martyred May 5, 1426,
and his relics were discovered January 3, 1950 after the Abbess
experienced a vision.

Access: Road: Located near Makri and the Mt. of Amomon.

Monastery of Agiou Ioannou Theologou Preveli
Preveli   Tel: 0832 31 246
74060 Myrthios
Kriti, Greece
Greek Orthodox

Open To: Monastery under reconstruction. Not open to
visitors at this time. Contact for further information.

Of Interest: This men's monastery was established in 1550
and played an important role during Kretan Wars. It was
destroyed during the Turkish War of 1646 and rebuilt in 1700
by the monk Iokovos (Jacob). The Church, dedicated to St. John
the Theologian and Evangelist, was remodeled in 1836 and
again in 1911. Special feastdays are celebrated May 8th and
September 26th. The monastery has many relics of saints and
holy artifacts and icons. It made an important contribution in
the field of elementary education during the 19th c.

Access: Road: Located 40 km. S of Rethimnon at the seashore,
past the villages of Asomatos, Lefkogeia, and Yianniou on the
Island of Crete.

Metohion Milesiou   Tel: 0295 98261
Milesi   Fax: 0295 98074
19015 Nea Palatia   Contact: Sr. Fevronia
Attikis, Greece
Greek Orthodox

Open To: Pilgrims for day visits. The Sisters speak only Greek.

Accommodation: None at present due to ongoing construction and remodeling. Contact for further information.

Guests Admitted To: Chapel. Grounds, including the last room of The Elder Porfyrios.

Of Interest: The Elder Porfyrios founded this house of peace – The Transfiguration of the Savior. His biography is available from the Sisters and is published in English. There are plans for Russian and French editions.

Access: Road: Located 4 km. from Athens in E Attica, East Central Greece opposite Euboea, the largest island of Greece.

Holy Church and Monastery of Panagia H Skripous
Orhomenou Voiotias   Tel: 0261 32211/33593
32300 Orchomenos   Fax: 0261 34092
Greece   Contact: Fr. Haralampos
Greek Orthodox   Hatziharalampous

Open To: Pilgrims/visitors wishing to view the famous church and monastery and attend worship services. Day visits year round.

Guests Admitted To: Byzantine-style Church (874 AD), built in shape of a cross. Other historic churches, including Agios Sozon (1010 AD), and Church of St. George (16th c.).

Of Interest: This sacred and ancient church, Ieros Byzantinos Naos, is in the process of restoration since an arson fire destroyed many portions. Two other names for the church are Apostolos Petros and Apostolos Pavlos. Special feastdays of the Panagia are August 23rd, with Vespers the preceding night, and September 10th, when the whole town celebrates having been spared from German occupation, with a Vesper service in the evening. On September 10, 1943, the Mother of God appeared in a cloud before the advancing German forces. As she raised her hand, the tanks stopped dead in their tracks, as though glued to the ground. The Commander Hoffman begged local citizens to help pull the tanks free with their tractors. As he knelt before the Icon of Panagia, he recognized in the painting the face of the woman whose sudden appearance immobilized the German Army. He insisted that the people of the town pay special homage to her for saving their city. This city has many historical sites from various periods.

Access: Rail: Service available. Road: Athens 120 km.

Holy Monastery St. John the Baptist   Tel: 0834 94 274
Iera Moni Atalis-Bali   Contact: Abbot
74057 Panormon Myl/Mou
Greece
Greek Orthodox
Metropolis of Rethymnon and Avlopotamos
Community of Melidonion

Open To: Visitors during the day, except Fridays. Modest
dress code. Respect must be shown for this hallowed ground.

Accommodation: None at this time due to ongoing
restoration, begun in 1983. Contact for further information.

Guests Admitted To: Two-aisled Monastery Church,
consecrated to St. John the Baptist. The older side (north) has
some frescoes, and is honored on June 24th, the birthday of its
patron saint. The south side is honored on Aug. 29th, the
feastday of the Beheading of St. John.

Of Interest: The monastery's original name comes from the
ancient town of Astali on the Gulf of Bali, Axos Harbor. Under
Turkish Rule, the name changed to Bali, perhaps because this
area has a wide variety of fragrant herbs and is known for its
production of honey (Bali means honeyplace). The monastery
flourished during the 17th and 18th c. The monks took an active
part in the fight for liberty in the Cretan Revolutions of the 19th
c. against the Turks. However, revenge against Atali-Bali
Monastery destroyed the Brotherhood except for a handful of
monks who remained on monastery grounds until 1941. Since
1983, there has been a resurgence of monastic life, and the
faithful have been assisting the monks with restoration efforts.

Access: Road: Km-stone 31 of the new national road
Rethimnon-Heraklion through a 500 m. roadway. Located on E
side of St. Hypakois Hill of Mt. Kulukunas near the settlement
of Bali.

Holy Apostles and St. Nektarios Monastery
Loukakia   Tel: 0297 32833
85500 Patmos, Greece   Contact: Guest Father
Greek Orthodox

Open To: Pilgrims, students for day visits, except Wed. and
Fri. For those seeking spiritual renewal and inner healing.
Monks available to hear Holy Confession and to give Spiritual
Direction. Guests are asked to respect the sacredness of this
hallowed ground.

Guests Admitted To: Church of St. Nektarios. Magnificent
icons depicting scenes of St. John's Apocalypse. St. John the
Apostle was exiled on the Island of Patmos where he was
blessed with visions of the End Times. Revelations, the last
book of the Bible, is ascribed to the Evangelist.

Of Interest: In the 17th c., a hermit (anchorite) lived a solitary
life in a cave on the islet of Plafi and built a small church in
honor of St. Luke the Evangelist. In the 18th c., a fisherman
named Pavlos found an icon of Panagia floating along the
seashore of Loukakia (small islets). In 1955, the Elder Pavlos
constructed three cells on this holy ground, and in 1968 the
small Church of St. Nektarios was built in Dodcanisa. Many
miracles have occurred from the Icon of St. Nektarios, housed in
the small church. A week prior to the Turks' invasion on
Cypress, the icon shed tears for days. Whenever there was a
conflict with Turkish forces, a fragrance would emanate from
the sacred image. In June, 1984 the Holy Elder Porfyrios
prophesied to elders Pavlos and Antipas that water would be
found at the foot of the mountain near the monastery. It was
found for the monastery in the Fall of that year.

Access: By boat, then by road. Patmos is located SW of Samos
in SE Aegian Sea.

Monastery Agiou Ioannou
Theologou Evangelistou
85500 Patmos
Greece
Greek Orthodox

Open To: Pilgrims/visitors.

Accommodation: Hospitality is provided in the monastery's guest quarters.

Guests Admitted To: Monastery Church (1088), built in the shape of a cross, with wall frescoes spanning the centuries. Magnificent wooden temple (1820). Wood carvings and icons (17th c.). Reliquary containing holy remains of Divine Christodoulos. Special Feastdays: Sept. 26th and May 8th – St. John; Mar. 16th and Oct. 21st – St. Christodoulos. Cave of Revelation. Church of St. Anna, Mother of the Virgin Mary, next to cave.

Of Interest: This men's monastery was founded in 1088 by the Divine Christodoulos Latrinos, a hermit on the Mt. of Latmos of Asia Minor who went to the Island of Kos in 1085 after having endured suppression from the Turks. It is built on the ruins of an ancient Christian Basilica of St. John the Theologian (4th c.), and the Basilica was built on the ruins of an ancient Church of Artemis. There are twenty monasteries on Holy Mt. Athos that resemble this one. They are built as a group of monasteries, surrounded by medieval walls, like fortresses. The Monastery of St. John the Theologian and Evangelist has many relics of saints, icons, and religious artifacts. Today, many villagers work at the monastery on the 'field of monks'.

Access: By boat to the Island of Patmos, then by road.

Iera Gynaikeia Koinoviaki   Tel: 061 459 058
Moni Agiou Nikolaou   Contact: Abbess
Mpala, Patron
T-TH 1219
26110 Patra, Greece
Greek Orthodox

Open To: Pilgrims/visitors for day visits.

Guests Admitted To: Church of St. Nicholas to participate in
the liturgical services of the monastery, only during the hours
the monastery is open. Send for current timetable. Special
Celebrations: Dec. 6th and May 10th.

Of Interest: The Monastery of St. Nikolaos (6th c.) was
originally a women's monastery and suffered much during times
of Turkish domination. In 1945, the monastery was re-
established again as a women's monastery. The buildings were
in a state of disrepair, and renovation work began in 1990,
under the guidance of Archimandritis Kyrillos. It is situated at
the foot of Mt. Panahaiko and has a lovely view of surrounding
areas, including the sea.

Access: Road: Located on the outskirts of Patras, District of
Syhainon, village of Mpala, on the Gulf of Patras, West Coast of
Greece.

Agios Ioannis Pelopiou
27060 Pelopio
Greece
Greek Orthodox
Holy Metropolis of Eleias

Tel: 06 24 31 393
Contact: Guest Sister

Open To: Pilgrims/visitors.

Accommodation: Hospitality is provided for one night for a few guests.

Guests Admitted To: Monastery Church, dedicated to St. John the Baptist. Holy Liturgy celebrated every Sunday. Special Feastday: June 24th.

Of Interest: This women's monastery, built in the early part of the 20th c., is situated in a country setting close to a river.

Access: Road: Located on the outskirts of the town of Pelopio, 17 km. from Pyrgos. Bus stops near the monastery.

Iero Proskynima
Osiou Ioannou Tou Rossou
34004 Prokopi
Evoias, Greece
Greek Orthodox

Tel: 0227 41206 (Lodging)
0227 41209 (Monastery)
Fax: 0227 41308

Open To: Pilgrims/visitors.

Accommodation: Hospitality is provided on monastery grounds.

Guests Admitted To: Byzantine-style Church of St. John the Russian (Agios Ioannis O Rossos) to join the monks for liturgical services. The saint's body lies at rest in an elaborate sepulchre.

Of Interest: St. John the Russian was born in the Ukraine in 1690. As a young man, he became a soldier of Peter the Great's army. He was taken prisoner by the Turks and brought to Constantinople, where they tortured him, calling him an infidel because he would not deny his Christian Orthodox faith. John met a martyr's death May 27, 1730 at the age of 40. Many miracles have been attributed to him while he lived and following his death. In 1924, with the population exchange between Greece and Turkey, refugees coming from Prokopio of Asia Minor brought the relics of St. John the Russian to Chalkis. They established the town of Neo Prokopio and built the Church, dedicated to the saint, between 1930-1951.

Access: By boat, then road, on Evoia, the largest island of Greece, in the Aegean Sea, NE of Attica and Boeotia in Central Greece.

Agios Georgios Lampetiou   Tel: 06 21 34 440
27100 Pyrgos   Contact: Guest Sister
Greece
Greek Orthodox
Holy Metropolis of Eleias

Open To: Pilgrims/visitors.

Accommodation: Hospitality is provided for one night for a few guests.

Guests Admitted To: Monastery Church, dedicated to St. George. Special Feastday: April 23rd. Grounds.

Of Interest: This monastery was remodeled for nuns in 1970. It is situated in an area of lush vegetation, vineyards, olive trees, pine trees and wildlife. It has many icons of St. George and other saints.

Access: Road: Gravel, winding uphill to the monastery. Located 2 km. from the village of Lampeti near Pyrgos on the coast, E of the southern tip of Zante Is.

Agios Nikolaos Frangopithimatos, Vounargo
TK27100 Pyrgos   Tel: 06 21 51 312
Greece
Greek Orthodox
Holy Metropolis of Eleias

Open To: Pilgrims/visitors for day visits.

Guests Admitted To: Monastery Church (1200), dedicated to
St. Nikolaos, for church services. Special Feastday: Dec. 6th.
Grounds of this ancient site.

Of Interest: According to tradition, a Greek named Frangos
was being pursued by Turks. He jumped from a rock onto his
horse, praying to St. Nicholas to spare him, and he was saved.

Access: Road: Located 12 km. from Pyrgos, between Vounargo,
Amaliada, and Pyrgos on the coast, E of the southern tip of
Zante Is.

Koimiseos Theotokou Skafithias   Tel: 06 21 94 273
TK27100 Pyrgos   Contact: Guest Sister
Greece
Greek Orthodox
Holy Metropolis Eleias

Open To: Pilgrims/visitors.

Accommodation: Hospitality is provided for up to 5 persons
for one night.

Guests Admitted To: Monastery Church for liturgical services
and to view the Icon of Our Lady of Skafithias. Special
Feastday: Aug. 15th. Museum. Library. Grounds.

Of Interest: According to tradition, the Icon of the Virgin of
Skafithias was lost, and a person of faith found it floating on the
waves near the seashore, and he created a place of worship to
honor the Virgin Mary. The Monastery of the Dormition of the
Virgin Mary Skafithias, founded in the 10th c., was once a men's
monastery. The monks suffered much during the various wars,
and were active participants in the Greek Revolution. Nuns
took over in 1970, and some remodeling has taken place since
then at this lovely place of prayer and peace.

Access: Road: Located near the village of Skafithia, 12 km.
from Amaliada and 18 km. from Pyrgos.

Moni Eisodiotissis
TK27100 Pyrgos
Greece
Holy Metropolis Eleias

Open To: Pilgrims/visitors for day visits.

Guests Admitted To: Monastery Church, dedicated to the Birth of the Virgin Mary. Special Feastday: Sept. 8th. Icon Workshop.

Of Interest: The stirrings of religious life began in a small rock cave nearby during the 15th c. Today this men's monastery retreat has a School of Icon Painting.

Access: Road: Located near the village of Agios Ioannis, 5 km. from the Road of Pyrgos to Katakolon.

Spiliani Monastery   Tel: 0273 61361
TK83100 Pythagorion   Contact: Guest Father
Island of Samos, Greece

Open To: Pilgrims/visitors for day visits to this small sanctuary hewn into the mountain. Guided Tour by one of the monks.

Guests Admitted To: The small Church in the Cave, dedicated to the Mother of God

Of Interest: Panagia Spiliani Monastery is located near the small town of Pythagorion, once the capital of the island, and within its ancient walls. The monks reside in a few small cells near the cave.

Access: By air or boat, then by road. Samos Is. is located in the Aegean Sea, off the W coast of Turkey.

Holy Monastery of Archangel Michael at Tharri
P.O. Box 722   Tel: 0244 61467
85109 Rhodes, Greece
Greek Orthodox
Holy Metropolis of Rhodes

Open To: Pilgrims, youth who wish to spend time in a monastic environment. Spiritual Direction available.

Accommodation: Hospitality is provided in the monastery's Guest House, which is also used as a summer camp for children.

Guests Admitted To: Church to join the monks for liturgical services. Grounds.

Of Interest: According to tradition, the Holy Monastery of Archangel Michael was founded by a Byzantine princess between the 9th and 10th c. She was healed of an incurable illness through the intercession of Holy Michael to whom she was especially devoted. She built the sacred church to honor Michael the Archangel, and in time the monastery buildings were added. It is situated on beautiful, peaceful wooded acres. Children from several countries have come here for Christian fellowship, and the faithful from around the world flock to this oasis of God's love. Besides missionary activities, the Brothers operate a radio and television station at Tharri. There are plans to establish the 'St. Cyprian Health, Healing and Convalescent Center for persons suffering from the stresses and strains of modern life.

Access: By road once on the island.

Iera Moni Skiadi
85100 Rhodos
Greece
Greek Orthodox

Tel: 0244 43006
Contact: Fr. Christian
Amphilochios Tsoukos

Open To: Individuals, groups, families wishing to visit the monastery and church, and for those seeking rest and renewal.

Accommodation: Hospitality is provided in the monastery's guest quarters.

Guests Admitted To: Church of the Panagias Skiadenis Rodou (1760), dedicated to the Mother of God. Special Feastday: Birth of the Virgin Mary – Sept. 8th.

Of Interest: Holy Monastery Skiadi was built in the early 1200's. The original altar now sets in the present church. The tomb of Priestmonk Ignatio Zanetidi, the founder of the newer church in the 18th c., is found at the church entrance.

Access: Road: Located near the village of Mesanagros, approx. 100 km. from the city of Rhodes at the opposite end of the island.

Agios Onoufrios Monastery
Gardelades
49083 Skripero, Corfu
Greece
Greek Orthodox

Tel: 0663 41160
Contact: Fr. Nicholas
Lefteriotis, Vicar of
Gardelades or
Onoufrios Committee at
0663 41573

Open To: Public for Mass, usually the first and third Sundays of the month and Feast Days. Also for a tour of the church. Day visits only.

Guests Admitted To: Monastery Church, dedicated to St. Onoufrios of Egypt. Church contains several works of are (iconostasis by the Corfiot artists Augustine the Hieromonk (19th c.) and Dionysios Sgouros (20th c.).

Of Interest: Agios Onoufrios Monastery was built in 1773 on the site of an old chapel. At present, no monks are in residence. It is administered by a committee of four members, one from each of four villages – Gardelades, Doucades, Skripero, and Upper Korakiana to whom it belongs. The monastery is under the Spiritual Authority of the Orthodox Bishop of Kerkyra and Paxos. Important icons, silver lamps, and precious holy vessels are kept in the village of Gardelades, and they are displayed in the church only on the Feastday of June 12th. The complex is situated on a hill of olive trees near the Ropa Valley.

Access: Road: Located 16 km. from the town of Corfu in the rural area of the village of Gardelades. Kerkyra (Corfu) is one of the Ionian Islands in the Ionian Sea off the SW coast of Albania in NW Greece.

Holy Monastery of the Transfiguration of Christ, Sagmata
Ypaton, Thebes   Tel/Fax: 0262 71249
P.O. Box 115
GR32200 Thebes, Greece
Greek Orthodox (New Calendar)
Diocese of the Bishop (Metropolitan) of Thebes and Levadia

Open To: Individuals seeking a time apart for rest and
renewal. Public welcome certain hours of the day.

Accommodation: Hospitality is provided for men in converted
monks' cells, with advance notice.

Guests Admitted To: Monastery Church (Katholikon) – 12th c.
Ruins of 7th c. Chapel of St. Basil the Great on monastery
grounds. Chapels of Holy Forty Martyrs, St. Nicholas, and
Osios Klimis (founder of monastery). Special Feastdays:
Transfiguration of Christ – Aug. 6th; Founder's Nameday – Jan.
26th and May 1st; The Exaltation of the Holy Cross – Sept. 14th.

Of Interest: This men's monastery was built around the 12th c.
due to the efforts of the monk Osios Klimis of Athens and with
generous donations from the Byzantine Emperor Alexios
A'Komninos. It sets on the ruins of the ancient temple of Ypatu
Dios (Supreme Zeus). The monastery has suffered much
plundering and devastation throughout its long history, and
many treasures were lost. Since 1970, it has undergone
restoration from the Brotherhood which settled here, and under
the guidance of the Metropolitan of Thebes and Levadia
Ieronymos. There are many relics here – the skull of Osios
Klimis, and a fragment of the Holy Cross, a gift from the
Emperor Alexios A'Komninos. Guests will enjoy beautiful views
of surrounding lakes and fields and peaceful walks to the small
forest nearby.

Access: Road: National Road from Athens to Lamia, exit at
70th km. to the parallel road leading to the village of Ypaton.
Located 6 km. from the village, uphill on a winding dirt road on
R side of the mountain.

Agia Eleoussa, Lygia   Contact: Guest Sister
TK27050 Vartholomio
Greece
Greek Orthodox
Holy Metropolis Eleias

Open To: Pilgrims/visitors wishing to view this small, ancient
monastery and cave in this place of prayer and peace.

Accommodation: Hospitality is provided for a few guests for
one night.

Guests Admitted To: Monastery Church for services and to
view the miraculous Icon of Eleoussa (Protector). Cave.

Of Interest: The Icon of the Virgin Mary was found in a cave
during the 9th c. The drops from the stalactites were believed to
be healing water. Worship services were originally held in the
cave. The monks helped the resistance during the Revolution.
In 1922, the Prime Minister gave part of the monastery to
refugees from Asia Minor to set up family life. Following WWII,
they felt it their duty to help the one remaining monk restore
the monastery. Nuns took over after the 1940's , and much hard
work and community involvement has gone into making
necessary improvements to the monastery and cave.

Access: Road: Located in a meadow NW of the village of
Vartholomio, 5 km. from the village of Lygia.

Holy Monastery Agiou Vlasiou Tel: 0743 91210
A.S. Trikalon Contact: Guest Sister
20400 Xylokastro, Greece
Greek Orthodox

Open To: Pilgrims/visitors wishing to pay homage to St.
Vlasiou and to learn more about the history of this monastery.
Spiritual Retreats.

Accommodation: Hospitality is provided for retreatants.
Overnight stays possible depending on availability of a room.

Guests Admitted To: Monastery Church (17th c.). Special
Feastday: St. Vlasiou – Feb. 11th. Icon Painting Room. Room of
historic artifacts and holy relics in the monastery. Gardens.

Of Interest: In the 14th c., a Christian found the Icon of St.
Vlasiou in a cave. He built a small church at the site, and later
relics of the saint were brought here. Today, the south end of
the monastery is near here. This was once a large monastery of
monks, but over time, only one dedicated monk remained as
caretaker. In 1924 it was in danger of closing when one nun
came to establish a women's monastery, and by 1928, several
more nuns had joined her. Today it stands as a Spirituality
Center.

Access: Road: Located in East Central Greek Peninsula.

Greek Orthodox Monasteries
Metropolis of Zakynthos

Agiou Ioannou Prothromou Langadas   Tel: 83442
Hartaton Katastariou
Island of Zakynthos, Greece

Open To: Day visitors.

Guests Admitted To: Church for liturgical services.

Of Interest: This ancient monastery was founded in the 16th c. After a period of disuse, it was restored in 1617. Presently, one monk resides here.

Access: By air or boat, then by road once on the island.

Yperagias Theotokou Hionata Kephallinias
Island of **Kephallinias**
Greece

Open To: Day visitors.

Guests Admitted To: Monastery Church. Grounds.

Of Interest: This new monastery is an annex of the Monastery Yperagias Theotokou Eleutherotrias.

Access: By road.

Agias Aikaterinis   Tel: 26362
Kipon
Island of Zakynthos, Greece

Open To: Day visitors.

Guests Admitted To: Monastery Church. Grounds.

Of Interest: This small monastery is an annex to a larger monastery.

Access: By road.

Metohi Yperagias Theotokou Yperagathou
Koiliomenou
Island of Zakynthos, Greece

Open To: Day visitors.

Guests Admitted To: Monastery Church. Grounds.

Of Interest: This small monastery is an annex to a larger monastery.

Access: By road.

Agios Georgios Krimnon   Tel: 31298
Krimnon
Island of Zakynthos, Greece

Open To: Day visitors.

Guests Admitted To: Monastery Church to join the monks for liturgical services. Grounds.

Of Interest: The Monastery of St. George was founded in 1535. At present, three monks are in residence.

Access: Road: Located in the vicinity of Volimon.

Monastery Yperagias Theotokou Eleutherotrias
Lagopodou   Tel: 92226
Island of Zakynthos, Greece   Contact: Guest Sister

Open To: Pilgrims/visitors wishing to spend time in a spiritual setting.

Accommodation: Hospitality is provided in the monastery's guest quarters for one night. Meals taken with the nuns.

Guests Admitted To: Monastery Chapel. Grounds.

Of Interest: This women's monastery was founded in 1961, and at present, there are approximately fifteen nuns in residence.

Access: By road.

Agiou Theotokou Spilaiotissis   Tel: 31218
Orthonion
Island of Zakynthos, Greece

Open To: Day visitors.

Guests Admitted To: Monastery Church for liturgical services.

Of Interest: This ancient monastery was founded in 1550 and is presently occupied by one Orthodox monk.

Access: By road.

Metohi Agiou Dionysiou   Tel: 0621 33210
Pyrgos Ileias
Island of Zakynthos, Greece

Open To: Day visitors.

Guests Admitted To: Monastery Church. Grounds.

Of Interest: At present, one monk is in residence at this small monastery.

Access: By road.

Metamorphoseos Strofathon and St. Dionysios Monastery
Zakynthos
Island of Zakynthos, Greece

Open To: Day visitors.

Guests Admitted To: Monastery Church. St. Dionysios Museum.

Of Interest: This is a men's monastery, located in the city of Zakynthos.

Access: By road.

Monastery of Anafonitrias
Island of **Zakynthos**
Greece

Open To: Day visitors.

Guests Admitted To: Monastery Church. Special Feastdays: Holy Martyrs of Strophathon – Sept. 30th; St. Dionysios – Dec. 17th; Celebration of transfer of St. Dionysios' relics to this island in 1717 – Aug. 24th.

Of Interest: This men's monastery is situated in the mountains. St. Dionysios (1547-1622) lived here as an ascetic, and is the patron saint of the island. His relics are kept in the gold room in the Church of Dionysios in Zakynthos.

Access: Road: Located on the west side of the island.

Turkey

St. Therese Chapel
Kardesler Sok. No. 15
06250 Ankara, Turkey
Roman Catholic

Tel: 0312 311 01 18
Contact: Parish Priest

Open To: Pilgrims/tourists – call beforehand to assure someone is available.

Guests Admitted To: Small Chapel (100 people) for Mass or private prayer.

Of Interest: St. Therese Chapel is located in a building owned by the French Embassy. There is no public church in Ankara, the capital of Turkey. The chapel is situated in the old part of town within two hundred meters of the Museum of Anatolian Civilizations (Archeological Museum).

Access: By rail or road; located in West-Central Turkey.

68

Catholic Church
Kurtulus Cad. Kutlu Sok., No. 6
P.K. 107
31002 Antakya, Turkey

Tel: 891 167 03
Fax: 891 418 51
Contact: Parish Priest

Open To: Pilgrims visiting Antioch who wish to stay in a
Christian Guest House.

Accommodation: Hospitality is provided in 6 bedrooms with
baths. Large self-catering kitchen, or meals taken at local
restaurants. Guests have their own key for convenience.

Guests Admitted To: Catholic Church for Mass and Evening
Prayer. Grotto of St. Peter, available for groups of pilgrims
upon request for Sunday Mass during principal feasts of the
Liturgical Year, and for special occasions. Local Orthodox
Church for Sunday Liturgy.

Of Interest: The historic city of Antioch has been a Province of
Turkey since 1939. It was here that the disciples were first
called Christians. Antioch was the point of departure for Paul's
first three Apostolic journeys, and Peter lived here for some
time before going to Rome. Today it is the titular seat of three
Catholic Patriarchs – the Syrian, Maronite, and Greco-Melchite,
and two Eastern Patriarchs – the Greek Orthodox and the
Syrian Jacobite. Pilgrims may wish to visit the ruins of the
Monastery of Simon the Stylite the Younger, twenty kilometers
from the city. The Grotto of St. Peter is located on the west
slopes of Mt. Stauris, one kilometer from the town center on the
Syrian Road. It was the meeting place of the first Christians.
In 1856 the Grotto was given into the keeping of the Capuchin
Fathers who have been present in Antioch since 1846.

Access: Road: Located in S Turkey in the Orontes Valley on
the slopes of Mt. Silipius, 25 km. from the Mediterranean.

Aghia Triada
Halki Island
Turkey
Greek Orthodox

Open To: Pilgrims wishing to visit this ancient site of monastic life.

Accommodation: None at the monastery or on the Island of Halki.

Guests Admitted To: Monastery Church (1896). Grounds.

Of Interest: The Monastery of the Holy Trinity dates back to the 9th c. Its long and often catastrophic history includes banishment of the monks in 820 in order for exiled members of royalty to reside here. St. Photios the Great, the true founder of the monastery, is the patron saint of its Theological School. During the 12th c., monasteries and convents of the Princes' Islands suffered destruction from enemies of the Orthodox Church. Aghia Triada was rebuilt in the 16th c. and renovated in 1844. Following the devastating earthquake of 1894, the complex was again rebuilt. The distinctive red-tiled roof is a prominent landmark. It is situated on the highest hill of the island. The Monastery of St. George by the Cliff lies to the south, and the Church of St. Nicholas is in the center of Halki.

Access: By boat, S of Istanbul.

St. George Koudounas Monastery
Halki Island
Turkey
Greek Orthodox

Open To: Pilgrims wishing to spend time in prayer at this ancient monastery. Day visits.

Guests Admitted To: Monastery Church (1906). Chapel. Holy Spring. Special Days of Pilgrimage: Feast of St. George – Apr. 23rd; Forty Days After Feast of the Dormition of the Virgin Mary – Sept. 24th.

Of Interest: The Monastery of St. George Koudounas dates back to the 10th c. It has suffered much destruction as a result of wars and natural disasters. According to tradition, a shepherd, while tending his flock on this mountainside, fell asleep and dreamed he heard bells ringing. He awakened and began to dig, finding an icon of St. George covered with devotional ornaments (tamata) and bells. It had been buried by iconophiles during the iconoclastic controversy to prevent its destruction.

Access: By boat. Located S of Istanbul in the eastern part of the Sea of Marmara.

Salesian Fathers   Tel: 212 248 09 10
Olcek, Sok. 82   Fax: 212 232 40 44
80230 Harbiye-**Istanbul,** Turkey   Contact: Father
                                       Defranceschi

Open To: Men and women seeking a quiet place for rest and
renewal. Closed to guests during June, July and August.

Accommodation: Hospitality is provided in a few rooms.

Guests Admitted To: Chapel. Garden.

Of Interest: This place of retreat is situated on the Island of
Buyuk Ada in the eastern part of the Sea of Marmara, W
Turkey, SE of the entrance to the Bosporus. It is the largest of
the Princes Islands.

Access: By boat, 1 hr. from Istanbul.

The Holy Stauropegial and Patriarchal Monastery of
    Zoodochos Peghe at Baloukli
34220 H. Fener-Istanbul
Turkey
Greek Orthodox

Open To: Pilgrims from around the world and people of all
faiths to pray at the ancient Shrine of Baloukli. Day visits.

Guests Admitted To: Orthodox Church (1833). Shrine and
the Hagiasma (holy spring). Special Feastday of the Life-Giving
Fountain on Friday of Bright Week.

Of Interest: His All Holiness Ecumenical Patriarch
Bartholomew is Abbot and Spiritual Father of this monastery.
According to tradition, this center of spirituality dates back to
the 3rd or 4th c. It has suffered much over the centuries from
invaders as well as from natural disasters, and it has been used
as a place of exile. A small church was built in the 18th c., and a
larger one was built in 1833, under the guidance of Patriarch
Constantius I. Today Orthodox Nuns from abroad are in
residence, some under the jurisdiction of the Ecumenical
Patriarchate. Restoration of the complex was completed in
recent years.

Access: Road: Located W of the city of Istanbul, outside the
Byzantine land walls.

Capuchin Fathers
Cumbus Sok. No. 8
34800 Yesilkoy-**Istanbul**, Turkey
Roman Catholic

Tel: 212 573 8294
Fax: 212 663 0337

Open To: Pilgrims – individuals and groups. Year round.

Accommodation: Hospitality is provided in a small hostel, which can cater to a max. of 20 persons. No meals on site.

Guests Admitted To: Chapel.

Of Interest: This Christian Hostel is situated in the village of Yesilkoy on the Sea of Marmara.

Access: Close to the airport, approx. 11.2 km. W of Istanbul.

St. Stephens Latin Catholic Church
Cumbus Sok. No. 8
34800 Yesilkoy-**Istanbul,** Turkey
Roman Catholic Capuchin

Tel: 0212 573 82 94
Fax: 0212 663 03 37
Contact: Pastor

Open To: Members of the Capuchin Order visiting Istanbul and also other priests and religious. Possibility of small groups accompanying priests while on pilgrimage.

Accommodation: Hospitality is provided in guest facilities of the convent in 10 single and 2 double rooms, all with baths. Other rooms could be made available for groups of young people.

Guests Admitted To: Catholic Church. Grounds.

Of Interest: The Convent of Yesilkoy-Istanbul, built in 1865, was completely remodeled in 1993, It is entrusted to Italian Capuchins, and many members of the Order are working throughout Turkey.

Access: Road: 4 km. from Istanbul Airport – near the sea.

Capuchin Fathers   Tel/Fax: 232892 60 08
Ephesus – The House of the Virgin
Meryemana Evi
35922 Selcuk-**Izmir,** Turkey
Roman Catholic

Open To: Men and women for Retreats.

Accommodation: Hospitality is provided in the Retreat
House. Meals included.

Guests Admitted To: Chapel. Grounds.

Of Interest: Izmir, one of the most important seaports in Asia
at the head of the Gulf of Izmir, has a large Greek population.

Access: By rail or road.

Mater Dolorosa Catholic Church   Tel: 0362 431 33 86
Bagdat cad N. 112   Contact: P. Brunissen
55030 Samsun, Turkey

Open To: Pilgrims/visitors for prayer and Mass. Day visits.

Guests Admitted To: Church for services.

Access: Good public transport. Located on the Black Sea.

Sancta Maria Katolik Kilisesi   Tel: 0462 321 21 92
Iskenderpasa Mah   Contact: Secretary
Sumer Sokak No. 26 PK 59
Trabzon, Turkey

Open To: Individuals, couples, small groups for rest and spiritual refreshment.

Accommodation: Hospitality is provided in the church complex in single and double bedrooms.

Guests Admitted To: Catholic Church for Mass and private prayer.

Of Interest: The historic coastal city of Trabzon has a number of Byzantine sites such as the Basilica of St. Sophia and many old churches. The Monastery Sumela, which is built into a cliff, is forty five kilometers from the city.

Access: Good public transport. Located on the Black Sea.

INDEX

Holy Michael, Archangel, defend us in battle and
protect us against the wickedness
and snares of the devil.
May God rebuke Satan, we humbly pray, and by
God's power may you, prince of the heavenly host
cast him into Hell with all the evil spirits who
wander through the world for the ruin of souls.

Amen